THE PRICE WE PAY . . .

Population Vs Immigration

THE PRICE WE PAY . . .

Population Vs Immigration

———

An examination by:
Virgil

ISBN-13: 9780578198538
ISBN-10: 0578198533
Printed in USA by 48HrBooks (www.48HrBooks.com)

Introduction

————

THE PRICE OF ANYTHING IS not always measured in dollars and cents. Occasionally, we are assessed a cost that we are unaware of . . . or worse – we think about it but ignore the consequences. Population, or I should say, excessive population and immigration (illegal or otherwise) are good examples.

Legislators, claiming to protect us, pass laws restricting human behavior. Recently, in California, legislation is being considered to penalize anyone looking at their cell phone while walking in an intersection because, *theoretically*, that behavior could endanger that person's life or involve a motorist in an accident because the pedestrian was not paying attention.

In June 2016, Governor Jerry Brown signed SB 277 into law. This bill nullified parental objections to vaccinations of their children except in cases of health issues or allergies. The logic is that parents simply are not qualified to make this kind of decision.

Mark Twain (1866) once remarked: "No man's life, liberty, or property is safe while the legislature is in session."

California passes more than one thousand laws every year – many of these laws seek to displace individual responsibility with legislative oversight.

There are indications populations in many industrialized nations could decline resulting from a reduction of fertility rates if it was not for a large influx of legal and illegal immigration. In 2014, the United States, for example, had an estimated fertility rate of 1.86 children per woman which is below the replacement fertility rate of 2.1; never-the-less, the U.S. population increased at a faster rate than most other countries.

Unauthorized or illegal immigration is currently a divisive issue in the U.S. and the potential price to be paid in terms of personal freedom or exposure to terrorism is yet unknown. Great Britain recently endured its' fifth terrorist event in September 2017; possibly a price paid for unrestricted immigration.

I have attempted to present an impartial examination of population and immigration issues in the hope that we, as a society, might recognize the *"The Price We Pay"* if we continue to ignore these problems.

CHAPTER 1

In The Beginning

IN AN ATTEMPT TO EXAMINE an issue or circumstance, ancient philosophers would often use a technique of drawing a circle and then proposing a situation which might occur exclusively in that circle. Accordingly, let us put a single person called "Adam" in that circle as a solitary human in a world of his own. This would have to be a special world which would include a warm climate and ample food.

To accommodate the food bearing plants, we give into this circle bees and insects to handle growth and spoilage. To limit the growth of insects, we supply birds and to hold down the population of birds, we put in some cats and to limit cats we grant life to dogs; to limit the dogs, larger predators are instituted. To reduce the growth of grass and shrubbery, we provide larger animals to graze the land. To eliminate carbon dioxide gasses, we provide trees to clean the air and provide a source of oxygen, and on it goes until a stable cycle of life is established because predator and prey are dependent upon each other to limit their existence in accordance to the food available.

Philosophically, a solitary person on the face of the earth is without restraint of any kind. He has no laws to follow, no problems with other humans and no restrictions, but is he truly free? We can surmise that most probably he would want companionship or a mate to share his life with; so let us give him "Eve" as a companion in life.

There is little doubt this circle of life becomes familiar to us an allegorical story from the first book of Moses called "Genesis" contained in the Holy

Bible as part of the Old Testament. It is a story of Adam and Eve as solitary humans within a "philosophical circle" called the garden of eden.

"And the Lord God planted. . .the tree of life: also in the midst of the garden, and the tree of good and evil . . . And the Lord God commanded the man, saying, Of every tree of the garden thou mayest freely eat: but of the tree of the knowledge of good and evil, thou shalt not eat of it: for in the day that thou eatest thereof thou shalt surely die.[1]*"*

As the story goes, the snake convinces Eve that she and Adam ought to eat of this fruit in defiance of the Lord God who commanded that they should not eat of it.

Within the true meaning of an allegorical story, this biblical tale has a hidden message or maybe even a warning for mankind.

A Buddhist Monk might conclude the garden of eden is about a form of utopia. Acceptance of what you have and the refusal to strive for more than you need leads to harmony with nature and all of the creatures living within.

Philosophically, one might conclude the true meaning is all of the above plus a warning that knowledge might lead to greed and avarice. The moral good is the acceptance of what you have.

A psychologist would note the fact a snake, often a symbol for the male penis when analyzing dreams, is the culprit in this tale. Possibly, this is a warning that sexual drive could lead to over-population and the destruction of nature's balance . . . *"in the day that thou eatest thereof thou shalt surely die."*

THE POPULATION COUNT.

Since there are no population records available during the cave man days, the earliest estimates (probably not based on actual count) begins with year number "1" AD. The term "AD" comes from the "Gregorian Calendar" (adopted by Great Britain in 1752), which is basically a Christian calendar because it uses the birth of Christ as a starting date: "BC" (before Christ) and AD (Latin *anno domini* "in the year of our lord").

Pulling up the *"World Population Clock[2]"* on the inter-net, in the year "1" AD, the world population was estimated at 200 million. From this starting date there are listed additional population milestones:

Year (AD)	Population count
1	200 Million
1804	1 Billion
1927	2 Billion
1960	3 Billion
1974	4 Billion
1987	5 Billion
1999	6 Billion
2011	7 Billion
2017	7.5 Billion
2023	8 Billion (estimated)
2040	9 Billion (estimated)
2056	10 Billion (estimated)

It is alarming to note that it took over 1800 years to go from 200 million to 1 billion in population, but only 16 years (2040 to 2056) to procreate 1 billion more residents on our planet.

In an attempt to translate billions of people on the face of the earth to a mathematical calculation that makes reasonable sense, the World Population Clock provides additional data which breaks down the population in numbers per square kilometer. This partial sample includes the eight most populated countries in the year 2017:

Country	*Population*	*p/Km²*	*(Km²)*
China	1,388,232,693	148	9,386,293
India	1,342,512,706	452	2,973,450
United States	326,474,013	36	9,144,930
Indonesia	263,510,146	146	1,811,066
Brazil	211,243,220	25	8,349,534
Pakistan	196,744,376	255	770,942
Nigeria	191,835,936	211	910,902
Bangladesh	164,827,718	1,256	130,175

For those of us who either refuse to accept the metric system or simply do not understand it, approximately 2.59 square kilometers equals one square mile. China's land mass of 9,386,293 Km² would equal 3.6 million square miles. Instead of 148 square kilometer, the density per square mile would be approximately 383. Since there are 640 acres in a square mile, there would be less than one person per acre in China based on the nearly 1.4 billion population figure. Even so, China introduced a "one-child" policy in 1979 in an effort limit population growth. This policy was phased out in 2015. China's population had continued to increase in any case.

Converting the numbers for Bangladesh to something we can understand, the density per square mile would be approximately 3,279 or a little more than five persons per acre, India's density would measure less than two persons per acre and the United States would have approximately one person for every six acres.

Clearly, a population count in comparison to land area does not reveal a realistic understanding of how human population works nor what would be a reasonable number of humans in accordance to the balance of nature.

We know, for example, that huge numbers of homo-sapiens congregate in large cities and that all countries have massive open spaces for food producing crops as well as forest areas, mountain ranges, desert areas and other land masses where humans do not or cannot dwell.

As a part of world population statistics,[3] New York City, for example, has an estimated 2016 population of 8,475,500 with a density of 27,807 people per square mile which calculates at 43 person per acre or one person per 1,000 square feet which would include streets and sidewalks. A family of four in the New York City Metropolitan area probably consider themselves lucky to have living accommodations of 1,000 square feet.

POPULATION: WHAT IS REASONABLE?

The movie "Soylent Green" (Charlton Heston – Edward G. Robinson) portrays a shocking future time on planet earth. As the story goes, the world population has exceeded the food available. Agricultural crops are only available to the privileged few and even the oceans are considered dead from pollution and relentless plundering of ocean life to handle the world food crises. Charlton Heston, in the course of his duties as a police officer, is pushing through crowded streets and constantly climbing over people in stairways of buildings. The shocking conclusion comes when he discovers that "Soylent Green" is food harvested from dead human corpses to feed the masses.

I think it would be safe to state this kind of population growth is not only unreasonable but unacceptable. The real question is what is a reasonable amount of people on the face of the earth?

A "Natural Law Philosopher" might point out that in nature when the population of a species of animal exceeds its' food supply, there is a massive die-off until the population matches the food available. In nature, excessive population is routinely solved without, it seems, any real fuss.

Historically, some areas of Africa routinely suffer from starvation. The human species, by bringing in food and shelter, apparently out of compassion, prevents the die-off of humans which would render a balance of population to available food. Accordingly, these over-populated areas, in an attempt to provide more food for their starving population, destroy large sections of the rain forest. These trees, once removed, can no longer scrub the air of Carbon Dioxide (C0-2) which, of course, contributes to carbon in earth's atmosphere.

Air pollution has always accompanied civilizations. Robert Angus, a Scottish chemist, discovered an atmospheric pollution called *"acid rain"* in 1852. Carbon dioxide emissions are causing ocean acidification and the decrease in the Ph of the Earth's oceans as vast amounts of C0-2 are absorbed in the world's oceans.

An innocent act of compassion, by failing to allow a starving human species to adjust its population in accordance to food available, sets in motion a loss of rain forest trees which are a part of nature's way of cleaning the air. This, of course, leads to a deterioration of earth's oceans, the loss of various forms of sea life which impacts those humans who depend on the ocean to provide food on the table.

CHAPTER 2

Excessive Population: *The price we pay*

———

LOSS OF FREEDOM.

ONCE AGAIN LET US DRAW a circle and then propose a situation which might occur exclusively in that circle. If we put a single person in that circle we can conclude he has absolute freedom to do anything he wants because there is no other person or animal to restrict his behavior. If we were to insert another person into the circle, this solitary human's freedom is reduced in accordance to the rights of this second person. A tribe or group setting not only limits individual freedom, but requires rules for tribal behavior and limitations of the rights of other tribes who venture into an established territory.

There is little doubt that the accumulation of humans in tribes, villages or cities requires those creatures living in this communal arrangement to give up their absolute freedom in favor of what works best for the group. This, of course, is the beginning of civilization.

LOSS OF IDENTITY

There was a time when the population of a town was small and everyone was acquainted with their neighbor and most other residents of their town. The local Mayor, even though elected, was not paid by public funds and the sheriff, a local man, was acquainted with most folks in town and was paid in accordance to his peace-keeping skills.

This small community has given way to a huge metropolis which includes residents who hardly know or even care about the vast majority of other occupants and everyone is held prisoner to the maze of streets and freeways on their way to and from some form of employment.

It is inevitable that unemployment or some form of misfortune leads to a dark and dismal community of homeless persons dependent upon the generosity of others in order to survive. These lost souls have become nameless digits on the city's general ledger where clerks record city expenses related to their stay.

But this loss of identity is not limited to the homeless; the city must account for all its residents. There are huge annual costs for city infra-structure, education requirements, police protection, health and payroll problems; hence, the city's residents are also reduced to digits on a data sheet of the city's general ledger. The family concerns and local gossip related to a small community, of which most people actually knew one another, no longer exists.

Back in the "good old days" only a small one-room school building was adequate to handle first through eighth grade students. The building and the necessary teacher could be acquired at a modest cost. Reading, writing and arithmetic with a little history thrown in was mandatory learning goals.

In the Modern world, after costing literally $-millions per year, some of these same first through eighth grade students manage to graduate but some cannot read, write or do fundamental math. One wonders if this is but another price we pay for ever increasing population numbers.

Us older folks can remember a time when small communities actually placed a welcome mat out for strangers to come and be a part of the community. Moreover, a brand new three bedroom, two bath (1,085 sq. ft.) house with a two car garage could be purchased for $16,000 or less. There were many two lane roads in those days, but traffic was "tolerable," as the saying goes.

Times have changed and the welcome mat has been replaced with a "keep out" attitude – not just in Monterey County (California) – but in nearly every community throughout our state.

More people means more traffic, more use of vital resources like water and then there is the pollution of the air we all breathe and the increase in garbage on our beaches and along our public roads.

Now we (as a community) have put up barriers to prevent population growth. There are endless requirements to be overcome by prospective builders like environmental impact reports justifying water use, air quality, additional traffic solutions, protection of unknown animal species "ad infinitum."

And if a project somehow gets past all this, there are impact fees, architectural reviews, permit fees and then, of course, the ultimate confrontation with planning commissions and city councils or county board of supervisors. But none of this covers the potential litigation put forth by the "smart growth" or "no growth" contingent.

Limiting population growth by creating barriers to prevent community development does not solve a state-wide problem, nor projected problems within the United States or the world for that matter. There appears to be a logical disconnect between anti-development in a local community and failure to perceive population as a problem elsewhere. Does it make sense to provide food to starving populations in third world countries without also making some effort to limit population in accordance to available food and water?

POLLUTION.

The New Century Dictionary printed in 1931 comes in two volumes for a total of more than 4,000 pages but, never-the-less, does not have the word "homo-sapien" listed anywhere in either volume. It does, however, have the word "Homo" meaning man and "sapiens" meaning the quality of being Sapient; wisdom; often used ironically.

Archaeologists have theorized these up-right, two-legged creatures ran around gathering fruit and nuts and living off the land. We presume the air was clean and the water so pure it could be consumed without injecting chlorine. There were no stop lights or traffic jams and no need for a 40-hour week, taxes, wars, robberies, sex crimes or terrorism. We do not know the life expectancy way back then, nor can we imagine the impact of disease and the bitter cold of winter, but we do know that a psychiatrist was not necessary in those days; nor hand grenades, machine guns, mustard gas or atomic bombs.

Considering this upright homo-sapien is supposed to possess some degree of wisdom, it might seem, after 250 thousand years, we would be blessed with more than fancy cars and flush toilets; instead, we are stuck with bad air, acid rain, crowded streets, stubborn, uncompromising politicians, and a never ending wars in foreign lands.

The world has had to live with acid rain; we are told our rivers, streams and fresh water sources are becoming polluted from human waste, insecticides and agricultural fertilizers. Even the oceans are suffering from pollution, over fishing and poor management which will ultimately lead to extinction of food sources and the balance of nature. We are informed the ozone layer is disappearing; hence, a rise in world temperature and a melt-down of the ice pack which may explain the unusual and violent weather and on and on it goes.

It is fascinating that many have reached a conclusion the human species is polluting the earth and fouling the air with carbon dioxide plus other noxious gases. These concerns have resulted in various theories and plans to correct the problem.

Not all that long ago there was a proposal (covered by the Fresno Bee[4]) that dairy cows were passing volumes of methane gas into the atmosphere. It was suggested these herds should be reduced. It is understood that while the offending herds are passing gas, literally thousands of cars are passing by discharging unknown quantities of pollutants into the air.

Politicians have proposed various tax solutions including an incredible "Cap and Trade" scheme to exact taxes from huge corporations who simply raise their rates so the consumer is the ultimate benefactor of the tax. And now many are suggesting we need a "back-up" plan in case all these brilliant plans, including "geo-engineering," might not work.

I hasten to add that, as a back-up plan, we might consider reducing the human population. There was a time, many years ago, when massive forests existed on the face of the earth including the rain forests of Africa and South America which scrubbed the air of CO_2. Of course, in those days the population was measured in the millions (not billions) and there was no need to cut down trees to provide land for food and living space.

Finger pointing and fault finding doesn't begin to address the real problem. There is little doubt that increased population, everywhere in the world, is resulting in huge demands on natural resources, food and water – not to mention the unpredictable human behavior that accompanies increased population growth.

THE POPULATION DILEMMA.

Obviously, the economic impact versus environmental consequences of population growth is the greatest dilemma of the modern era. Capitalism, recognized as the economic system utilized by the world's industrialized nations, is dependent upon Population. A capitalistic economy requires consumers – more people mean more potential customers. Moreover, mass production coupled with the stock market requires big business to show profits on an increasing basis every year.

To insure increased sales, the manufacturer produces a product with a limited life expectancy resulting in a future replacement. The technology industry markets new and improved computers, cell phones and television sets to continue an increasing sales strategy. Accordingly, many products on the market today require replacement instead of repair.

Big business has benefitted from increased population, but now there is a new problem to overcome. Originally, employers complained about the cost and inconvenience of withholding employee taxes, paying SDI, a share of social security, workman's compensation and State-Federal unemployment Insurance.

Employers may very well look back on these simple duties as the good old days. State and Federal legislators have tacked on minimum wage laws, pension benefits, health insurance, emergency duty leave, military leave, paid family leave, pregnancy leave, sick leave, nursing mothers – just to name a few of an increasing array of employer responsibilities.

Now, under increasing State and Federal legislation, employees have become very expensive. On the one hand big business desires cheap labor and might even admit "off the record" that an illegal work force is cheap and desirable because they cannot complain to anyone for fear of deportation.

On the other hand, slave labor is repugnant to American moral standards not to mention that it has been outlawed since the civil war.

Automation in the work place appears to be an employer solution. A robot requires no employee benefits and stabilizes product cost. Self-check-out stands are appearing in grocery and retail shops. It is difficult to estimate how many jobs are being lost, but automation as a solution creates another problem. The dilemma is the consumer has to be employed in order to purchase the product these businesses are selling. It is difficult to imagine how the ever increasing population will be able to get employment when automation is specifically designed to eliminate the expense of employees.

THE NOT-SO-BRAVE NEW WORLD.

It is reasonable to conclude most large employers – which would include agriculture – will go to automated equipment which would include robots. This, in turn, would result in a large segment of unemployed persons. Certainly a step toward the science fiction scenario of a "Brave New World" as well as the crowded streets and stairways described in "Soylent Green."

An Associated Press article by Cathy Bussewitz[5] entitled "Fear of robots taking jobs spurs a bold idea," explores the idea of universal basic income as a solution to increased technological innovations and robots that render large portions of the population unemployed and without income.

According to this article, programs to provide basic income are already in progress. The Economic Security Project committed $10 million over two years for basic income projects and a trial program in Kenya funded by "GiveDirectly," a U.S. group, has been started.

Providing basic income to expensive countries like the U.S. would require a huge reserve of funds. It was estimated that to give Hawaii residents $10,000 per year would cost $10 billion a year.

Historically, a socialized economic system has been criticized by proponents of an open market and free trade. Social security and unemployment insurance, during the Franklin D. Roosevelt administration, was criticized as socialism.

Thomas Jefferson, one of this nation's founding fathers, had little use for governmental intrusion in private affairs:

> *"The democracy will cease to exist when you take away from those who are willing to work and give to those who would not. I predict future happiness for Americans if they can prevent the government from wasting the labors of the people under the pretense of taking care of them."*

Population in the 18th century United States could be counted in the thousands; hence, Jefferson could not possibly imagine the huge numbers of people populating the earth in today's world. Even so, the real question is: *"Does this nation want to resort to a society totally dependent upon government controlled hand-outs?"*

CHAPTER 3

OVER-POPULATION: *What can be done?*

THE ONE-CHILD POLICY – WIKIPEDIA[6].

CHINA, IN 1979, INTRODUCED A one-child policy as a part of their "family planning," but phased it out in 2015. The policy had many exceptions. Ethnic minorities were exempt, and a little over one-third of the population was held to strict adherence to the policy leaving more than half of the remaining population the option to have a second child if the first child was a girl. Provincial governments imposed fines for violations.

The Chinese government claimed that more than 400 million births were prevented. Some scholars, however, question this statement pointing out that since 1979, the fertility rate had already declined in China. Fertility rates had also declined in Thailand, Iran and the Indian states of Kerala and Tamil Nadu without a one-child policy.

It would appear a "one-child" policy is subject to exceptions, cheating on the part of parents and heated debate by those concerned about passing on the family name and traditions.

A two-child policy was adopted on October 29, 2015 according to a statement from the Communist Party of China.

A QUESTION OF CONTRACEPTIVES.

Various forms of contraceptives were offered and recommended by the United States to areas which historically suffer from over-population. Some provinces of Africa refused to accept the contraceptive idea unless the U. S. also consented to use the same contraceptives they were recommending to the rest of the world.

Based upon all the rhetoric concerning why abortion should not be allowed as part of any government insurance benefit, it is doubtful the U.S. leadership would consider an aggressive program of contraceptive use to limit population. The Catholic Church has historically been inflexible with respect to its abhorrence of any "unnatural" technique to avoid pregnancy. This ideology has been extended to Africa where huge populations starve on an annual basis. The irony is many conservationists urge something be done to prevent these same starving peoples from cutting down the forest in order to grow crops to feed themselves. Various unusual and rare plants, birds and animals are at risk of becoming extinct because of deforestation and the large stands of trees in Africa and South America help clean the air which benefits populations around the globe.

It would appear that our world environment is being plundered and over-run by thoughtless creatures who are supposed to have superior intelligence. Based upon all the rhetoric concerning whether or not our insurance carrier "ought" to be required to cover abortions and/or contraceptives so as to resolve unwanted pregnancies, one might ask "is our planet running short of these two legged, upright homo-sapiens?" Moreover, if we allow indiscriminate use of these preventive devices, will humans become extinct? Obviously, someone must think so because no one is complaining about insurance coverage of Viagra and other potions which are designed to enhance sexual activities.

The Right to Die

When discussing the "Right to Die" legislation that "S" word (suicide) keeps popping up as if any legislation that might relieve persistent and agonizing pain of a loved one is a form of suicide and therefore despicable!

They shoot horses don't they?!

Childhood hop-along Cassidy westerns portrayed the heroic cowboy as being compassionate and thoughtful when putting to death his trusty horse to prevent pain and suffering of a broken leg or other disabling injury.

It is not that unusual for a pet owner to put down his favorite dog or cat if it is determined the health issue will result in a lingering death sentence.

But somehow, when it comes to family members who, in many cases, have given us life, provided us with loving care, food and shelter, but who, in their declining years, have fallen prey to some terrible end of life ailment; well, they must be prevented from getting relief from their pain and suffering because that would be a form of suicide.

I might mention the movie "Soylent Green" (Charlton Heston – Edward G. Robinson) which offered a simple and effective way to end it all when a person gets tired of living. The American society abhors this solution, but it is a better alternative than some crazed individual who loads himself up with a bomb and kills everyone around him – or a person who commits suicide by cop.

In any case, it is time for this society to give our "human" loved ones the same respect we reserve for our pets.

POPULATION CONTROL BY NATURE?

It is well established that predators such as lions and tigers present little threat to the human species; however, one wonders if it is possible that some other natural phenomenon might reduce the world's burgeoning population?

There is evidence that infinitesimal critters in the form of infectious diseases have resulted in mass deaths throughout history. These infectious diseases, which are spread through a human population over a large geographical area, are referred to as "Plagues" or "Pandemics."

PLAGUES AND PANDEMICS[7].

Because we live in an era where travel to anywhere in the world is fast and relatively inexpensive, the possibility that someone might be exposed to some sort of infectious and readily transmittable virus, which could be passed on to others resulting in a worldwide pandemic, is a real possibility.

Historically, pandemics are nothing new. There is evidence of a plague or possible pandemic more than two thousand years ago called "the Plague of Athens" 430 BC. The exact cause of this plague is not known but typhoid fever is suspected; never-the-less, over a period of four years, one quarter of Athens' population died.

Smallpox, a contagious disease caused by the variola virus, is thought to have made its first appearance in 165-180 AD and is termed the "Italian Plague." This disease resulted in 300-500 million deaths during the 20th century and as late as the 1950's an estimated 50 million cases of smallpox occurred worldwide each year. According to the World Health Organization, vaccination campaigns throughout the 19th and 20th centuries, eradicated smallpox by the end of 1979. To this day, smallpox is the only human infectious disease to have been completely eradicated.

Bubonic Plague, also known as the *black death*, was first recorded from 541-to-750 AD. It started in Egypt, and reached Constantinople the following spring, killing (according to the Byzantine chronicler Procopius) 10,000 a day at its height.[7] During the Middle Ages (1347-1453), this plague returned to Europe and resulted in an estimated worldwide death toll of 75 million people. Starting in Asia, the disease reached Mediterranean and western Europe in 1348 and killed an estimated 20 to 30 million Europeans in six years; a third of the total population. China and India suffered from the Bubonic plague beginning in 1855 resulting in 10 million deaths. The United States had it's first outbreak in San Francisco between 1900-to-1904 and isolated cases of the plague are still found in the western U.S.

Influenza was first described by Hippocrates, a Greek physician and father of the "Hippocratic Oath," in 412 BC. Apparently, the first influenza pandemic was recorded in *1580,* and since then, influenza pandemics occurred every 10 to 30 years. Pandemics of note are the "Russian Flu" (1889-1890), the "Asian Flu" (1957-58), and the "Hong Kong Flu" (1968-69). Probably the influenza outbreak that most affected the United States was the "Spanish flu" (1918-1919). There is little doubt the spread of this flu was expedited by returning soldiers from World War I. By October 1918, it had spread to become a worldwide pandemic on all continents, and eventually infected about one-third of the world's population (or 500 million persons).

HIV - AIDS originated in Africa, and spread to the United States between 1966 and 1972. HIV stands for human immunodeficiency virus. It weakens a person's immune system by destroying important cells that fight disease and infection. There is no effectlve cure for HIV but it can be controlled with proper medical care, education about safer sexual practices and blood-borne infection precautions.

The AIDS virus is considered a pandemic because it has spread by a human population over a large geographical area with infection rates as high as 25% in southern and eastern Africa. The AIDS death toll in Africa may reach 90-100 million by 2025.

Other Pandemics and Plagues of note: - Syphilis, Cholera, Typhus, Measles, Tuberculosis, Leprosy, Malaria, Yellow fever, Diphtheria and even Tetanus.

Incredibly, all of these afflictions have resulted in some form of pandemic or plague killing millions. If the reader desires additional information, I would suggest "Pandemics" by Wikipedia[7] (obtained on the internet) which offers a thorough analysis.

Troublesome Viral infections.

In recent years there have been serious outbreaks of "viral hemorrhagic fevers" such as the Ebola virus, Lassa fever virus, Rift Valley fever, Marburg virus and Bolivian hemorrhagic fever which are highly contagious and deadly diseases. Currently, their ability to spread efficiently enough to cause a pandemic is limited because the transmission and spread of these viruses requires close contact with infected victims. There is a fear, however, that genetic mutations might occur which could lead to a more transmittable virus and cause widespread disaster.

Antibiotic resistance microorganisms or "Super Bugs" are probably the most significant health care issue of the modern world. Antimicrobial Resistance (AMR) occurs when a microbe or bacteria develops resistance to medication used to treat them. Many hospitals are resorting to more and more powerful anti-biotics in treatment of infections; moreover, some cases of

AMR are resistant to the most powerful drugs available leaving the medical profession without an effective cure.

Medical professionals will tell you that antibiotic resistance can develop by genetic mutation (one species acquiring resistance from another), or by random mutations, but the most common cause of these super bugs is the gradual buildup over time due to misuse of antibiotics or antimicrobials.

"Superbugs" may contribute to the re-emergence of diseases which are currently well controlled. Currently, some cases of tuberculosis are found to be resistant to traditionally effective treatments which is cause for great concern to health professionals. It is estimated that nearly half a million new cases of multidrug resistant tuberculosis (MDR- TB) occur each year on worldwide basis. The World Health Organization (WHO) reports that approximately 50 million people worldwide are infected with MDR TB, with 79 percent of those cases resistant to three'or more antibiotics.

Flesh-eating Bacteria known as ***Necrotizing Fasciitis,*** is another modern day medical nightmare. It is unknown if advanced miracle drugs have somehow led to this new development of aggressive bacteria, but one can theorize that the cave man probably did not suffer from it.

On the positive side, flesh-eating bacteria is considered rare, but every year, between 600 and 700 cases are diagnosed in the U.S. and the fatality rate for victims of this disease is between 25% to 30%. The primary cause of this bacterial disease is group "A" Streptococcus or the same type of bacteria that causes strep throat. It can enter the body through minor cuts, insect bites, abrasions and/or surgery.

According to the Center for Disease Control (CDC), catching *Necrotizing Fasciitis* from someone else is extremely rare and the best defense against getting the disease is a healthy immune system. This flesh-eating disease is more common in people who have chronic health issues which weaken the immune system. The medical treatment for this disease involves intravenous antibiotic therapy and surgery to remove damaged or dead tissue. Severe cases can result in amputation of affected limbs, blood transfusions and intravenous immunoglobulin to assist the body's ability to fend off the disease.

SARS, an acute respiratory syndrome, was first identified in 2003 by Carlo Urbani, an Italian physician, who became infected and died from the very disease he identified. This new and dangerously contagious disease is caused by a *coronavirus* dubbed SARS-CoV. Rapid action by the World Health Organization and international health authorities broke the chain of transmission, which ended the localized epidemics before they could become a pandemic. It should be noted this disease has not been eradicated. It could re-emerge.

CHAPTER 4

Can Nature control population?

––––––

IT IS INTERESTING TO NOTE statistics provided by the World Health Organization (WHO) indicates the top ten most deadly diseases afflicting the African continent is: Pneumonia, HIV (Aids), Malaria, Diarrhea, Tuberculosis, Measles, Whooping Cough, Tetanus, Meningitis and Syphilis; whereas, in the more advanced industrial nations, these diseases are effectively controlled either by medication or through the use of vaccines.

Another surprising fact is that the Ebola Virus and the Viral Hemorrhagic Fever are not listed in the top ten deadly diseases for which neither has a known cure and is treated by isolating victims to prevent spread of the disease which exacts a high death toll.

The irony is that most advanced industrialized nations have a falling fertility rate, but those areas most afflicted with a variety of more common diseases have a high birth and an increasing population rate such that it would appear the theory of population control by nature does not work. A review of "The Population Count," listed earlier, reveals that population may be temporarily reduced by various plagues and pandemics, but has continued to increase at a remarkable rate throughout recorded history.

FERTILITY RATES ARE FALLING.

The question concerning what can be done to bring human population into balance with food available may already be in the process of solving itself. According to a Wikipedia demographic study[8], the U.S. fertility rate estimated for 2014 was 1.86 children per woman which is below the replacement fertility rate of 2.1 (approximately). In 2012, US fertility rate was lower than that of France (2.01), Australia (1.93) and the United Kingdom (1.92).

The fact that U.S. population growth is the highest of any industrialized nation is due to immigration which more than offsets the declining fertility rate.

There is little doubt that population control is a matter to be solved by human planning and intelligence. A declining fertility rate will not solve over-population if other areas engage in unlimited child birth and migrate to less populated areas. The immigration issue will be discussed later.

CHAPTER 5

Medical Research and Vaccinations.

———

AN ARGUMENT CAN BE MADE that increased population has resulted in better living conditions for the majority of the human species including many medical innovations which have reduced human suffering and prolonged human life which, accordingly, has resulted in increased numbers of humans. Penicillin and a host of anti-biotics has saved lives from infectious diseases and a vaccine, as previously mentioned, has completely exterminated small pox not to mention the benefits of the polio vaccine, influenza shots and countless others.

MANDATORY VACCINATIONS.

Historically, plagues and pandemics have visited upon societies everywhere on earth horrendous death tolls with no hope of a cure. It would naturally follow that if a means to prevent a disease, in the form of a vaccination, was discovered that it would seem unnecessary to pass legislation requiring universal participation.

All 50 states and the District of Columbia have vaccine requirements[9] which have to be fulfilled prior to attending public schools which includes kindergarten. California state law requires evidence of vaccinations for: Polio, Diphtheria, Tetanus, Whooping Cough (Pertussis), Measles, Rubella (German Measles), Mumps, Hepatitis B, and Chicken Pox (Varicella).

In early 2015, a highly infectious measles virus infected 162 people in 17 states of which at least 119 were in California. California is one of 19 states which allowed exemptions from vaccinations based purely on parents' personal or religious beliefs. The question arose as to whether a parent had the right to refuse vaccinations for their children in view of the possible spread of this infectious disease.

It could be argued that, in "the old days," there were no vaccinations for measles, rubella, whooping cough, mumps or chicken pox and those who came down with these diseases were quarantined. If they survived, they were immune for the rest of their lives. Today, with modern medicines, these same diseases do not pose a serious threat; whereas, eliminating the parent's right to determine what can and cannot be done to their children is a serious threat to personal freedom. Moreover, it has been subsequently discovered that vaccinations are only a temporary defense which means they require booster shots later in life and they are not 100% effective when and if taken.

Additionally, it is argued that mass vaccinations are the leading cause for the dynamic increase of the Autism Spectrum disorder. Medical professionals deny this argument stating that extensive research shows that thimerosal (a chemical included in some vaccines which contains mercury) does not cause autism.

The California State legislature refuted all arguments by passing SB 277 in June, 2015 which denies parental rights to object to vaccinations unless they can provide medical evidence of possible harmful consequences.

MIRACLE DRUGS.

Penicillin, considered a miracle drug, was the first of many revolutionary drugs developed in the 20th Century. The advent of research laboratories and the growth of large pharmaceutical firms began to appear to satisfy mass appeal for a quick and effective cure of every conceivable human ailment. Those cases which could not be treated by a pill or a shot, vaccinations have been developed.

Some human ailments are not solved by a vaccination which has given rise to research of the Human Genome and techniques to splice the DNA or develop human parts in the laboratory. Some might suggest this development is all too similar to the science fiction novel "Brave New World" featuring test tube babies designed to fulfill specific job tasks required by the modern society.

In August of 2017, the Food and Drug Administration (FDA)[10] approved, for the first time, a treatment that uses a patient's own genetically modified cells to attack a type of leukemia, opening the door to what the agency calls "a new frontier" in medicine. This process, known as CAR T-cell therapy, is designed to be used in children or young adults fighting an often fatal recurrence of the most common childhood cancer: B-cell acute lymphoblastic leukemia.

Unfortunately, the therapy can have dangerous side effects -- mainly a condition known as cytokine release syndrome. That happens when T cells release a lot of a chemical messenger into the bloodstream. This affects the vascular system, causing high fevers and sharp drops in blood pressure. More than 60 of patients in clinical trials had side effects due to cytokine release, but none of those reactions were fatal.

Another alarming concern is the price tag of **$475,000** associated with the "CAR T-cell" therapy**.** Even if the dangerous side effects are solved, how many persons can afford the cure?

THALIDOMIDE.
Even though Thalidomide is not a vaccination within the meaning of this sub-chapter, it is included here because not all modern medications proved to be without serious and sometimes fatal complications.

Some may recall the terrible consequences resulting from *"thalidomide"* which was developed in the United Kingdom back in 1958. It was prescribed for treatments such as insomnia, morning sickness and depression. By 1961 it was pulled off the market because it was found to be a leading cause of birth defects in newborn babies. There were approximately 10,000 babies born worldwide who either had shortened arms or legs, or no limbs at all resulting from pregnant mothers who had used this drug.

It should be noted that the Federal Drug Administration had received considerable praise for not approving its use in the United States.

CHAPTER 6

Feeding the masses: the price we pay.

———

IT IS AN IRONIC TWIST of fate that, as the population grows and consumes more land, there is less remaining land to grow crops.

The Monterey Herald[11] carried an article entitled *"Monterey County Crop Values Down in 2016,"* in which Jim Bogart (president and general counsel for the Grower-Shipper Association of Central California) was quoted as saying: *"By 2050 farmers must produce twice as much food with one half the land that we have now."*

Farmers, in an effort to cut costs but provide a greater crop yield, have resorted to a variety of agricultural measures which includes genetically modified crops. Livestock and poultry farmers utilize agricultural waste as a feed mix for livestock and poultry.

Silage, often used in the feed for livestock is comprised of vegetable waste or residue left over from harvesting crops. It is gathered up and thrown into pits which, after it is covered up, creates tremendous internal heat from fermentation and emits a severe odor. The process creates a molasses flavored supplement for livestock feed but which can cause diarrhea if fed in large quantities.

At one time, some cattle feed lots included remnants of cattle parts as part of the feed regimen.

MAD COW DISEASE.

In the 1970's there was a horrific outbreak of "Mad Cow Disease" in the United Kingdom where more than 184,500 cases were noted in cattle. This disease is more properly known as *bovine spongiform encephalopathy (BSE)*. It is a progressive neurological disorder caused by an infectious transmissible agent termed a prion. When first identified, television coverage revealed a horrific scene with cattle staggering about, lacking in muscle coordination.

Fortunately, the United States identified (through 2015) only four cattle infected with mad cow prions and Canada identified 20 cases. Causes for this affliction is not entirely understood, but apparently, it was a practice to include in cattle feed remnants of cattle parts and human derived compounds. This practice has subsequently been banned. The on-going prevalence of mad cow disease in the U.S. and Canada is considered to be low but continues to be under surveillance.

CREUTZFELDT-JAKOB DISEASE (CJD).

There is a terrifying relationship of *BSE* to the human prion disease is called *Creutzfeldt-Jakob disease (CJD)*. Most cases of CJD occur spontaneously but exposure to brain or spinal tissues from an infected person may also result in the spread of this disease. There is no specific treatment or cure for this disease.

THE NATURAL FOOD TREND

Currently, many in the U.S. have developed a preference for so-called *"ORGANIC"* or *natural foods*. There is an increasing abhorrence of those foods grown with the use of powerful fertilizers or pesticides and many consumers fear genetically modified organisms (GMO) or the use of anti-biotics in livestock or poultry.

It is probable that this modern movement toward natural foods is a result of fear caused by "Flesh-Eating" bacteria and the terrifying threat of "Super Bugs" which have developed a resistance to anti-biotics – more commonly known as "Antimicrobial Resistance."

We can logically calculate that as the population grows, there is less land available to produce crops. Farmers, in an effort to provide food for an ever-increasing world population, have resorted to genetically modified plants which are resistant to adverse weather and various crop eating insects. Cattle feed lots, to hold down livestock losses, have resorted to modest use of antibiotics which many feel contribute to *Antimicrobial Resistance.* Poultry farms and egg laying farmers are not excluded from this practice.

CHAPTER 7

Man: The predator.

———

No study of population is complete without a look at the two-legged upright homo-sapien called "man" – a term which includes the male and the female of the species. There is little doubt "man" is the top predator on earth; no other animal or beast can compete or otherwise dispose of this two-legged creature – including (as previously noted) those pesky little viruses which have resulted in horrific plagues and pandemics.

Ignoring pollution and the destruction of earth's climate, (the obvious manifestations of his stay on earth), "man" is a predator with an appetite for domination and control of others. Historically this unpredictable side of man's nature has led to conflicts and wars thus reducing the population by millions over the years.

Once again, by looking at the population chart, it appears that even the act of war has not effectively reduced population; however, it should be noted that man has contrived weapons so powerful and destructive that he is now capable of destroying all life on the face of the earth. The nuclear age began when two powerful bombs were dropped on Japan and for the past 70-plus years society has had to live with the notion the world might come to an end with each new threat of war.

NIHILISM

The Webster's Seventh New Collegiate Dictionary defines Nihilism: " *A viewpoint that traditional values and beliefs are unfounded and that existence is senseless and useless . . . A doctrine or belief that conditions in the social organization are so bad as to make destruction desirable for its own sake independent of any constructive program or possibility."*

I have viewed with open-mouthed shock and dismay when seeing or reading news accounts of some young person, loaded with explosives, not only terminated his own life, but killed and mutilated all those around him when releasing the powerful explosives in a public place.

Is it proper to theorize that conditions are so bad in the Middle East that life has lost its meaning which justifies self-destruction and the elimination of others in the process?

I think we can conclude that population – or over-population – is, at least, a contributing factor to the feeling that life is not worth living; therefore, there is nothing to lose by self-destruction which would include everyone in the vicinity.

POPULATION: NOTABLE WARNINGS.

Referring to an interesting book *"Maps of Time"* by David Christian, he writes:

*"In 1960, an attempt to calculate the mathematical tendency of global population in the past 2,000 years concluded that human populations would reach infinity on Friday 13 November 2026. This calculation **(which came to be known as the 'doomsday equation')** is a reminder that such rates of growth cannot be sustained forever. In 1000 CE (common era) the world's population stood at about 250 million. At the end of the twentieth century, it had multiplied twenty-four times, to reach 6 billion. . ."*

"Humans have become," as Lynn Margulis and Dorion Sagan put it, *"a sort of mammalian weed."*

It should be noted the population as of September 1, 2017 is estimated at 7.5 billion.

POPULATION VS IMMIGRATION.

There is little doubt that population and immigration are part of the same problem. A solution to one cannot be achieved unless the other is also resolved.

CHAPTER 8

IMMIGRATION.: *The real issue.*

———

WHEN IT COMES TO U.S. Immigration, it appears "we" – Federal, State and local officials - are very good at ignoring the law. To begin with, it is offensive, apparently, to use the term "illegal alien." Instead, it is considered good manners to refer to the millions of persons residing in this country, in violation of our immigration laws, as "undocumented immigrants."

This word "undocumented immigrant" – what does that mean? The Webster dictionary describes an immigrant as someone who comes to a country with the intent to take up permanent residence, and undocumented means he did not fill out any papers to get here or to stay here; hence, he is here illegally. An "Alien," on the other hand, is a foreign born resident who has not been naturalized and is still a subject or citizen of a foreign country; accordingly, we might conclude an undocumented immigrant is really a nice way of saying "illegal alien".

According to an Associated Press news article by Alicia A. Caldwell[12], *"Thousands of immigrant children fleeing poverty and violence in Central America can cross alone into the United States and live in American cities."* Apparently, the driving force behind this movement is the recognition, throughout Honduras, Guatemala and El Salvador, that children who make the dangerous trip can effectively remain in the U.S. for years before facing even a moderate risk of deportation.

One can theorize that, if the average person came home one day to find that some stranger had committed trespass and violated the privacy of his home, there is little doubt this person would be requested to leave at once! The fact a person may be carrying a child and is making a claim her neighborhood is overrun with dangerous and illegal activity does not justify the illegal act of trespass.

If you cross the North Korean border illegally, you get 12 years hard labor. If you cross the Afghanistan border illegally, you get shot. Two Americans just got eight years for crossing the Iranian border. If you cross the U.S. border illegally, you get a job, a driver's license, food stamps, a place to live, health care, housing, child benefits, education, and a tax free business for 7 years?

It appears part of "our" immigration problem revolves around the question: "Do *'we,'* as American citizens, consider the boundaries of the United States to be part of our home?" The reluctance to immediately extricate or otherwise remove persons guilty of trespass into the U.S. is the real issue here!

Anchor Babies – also referred to as Jackpot Babies.

In a study provided by Wikipedia entitled *"Anchor Babies,*[13]*"* Utah Attorney General Mark Shurtleff is reported as declaring: "The use of the word 'anchor baby' when we're talking about a child of God is offensive." Never-the-less, the term anchor babies (and sometimes referred to as "Jackpot Babies") has stuck as a reference to babies born to illegal alien mothers who have given birth to a child within the borders of the United States in the hopes the child will act as an anchor that pulls the illegal alien mother and eventually a host of other relatives into permanent U.S. residency.

In another Wikipedia study entitled "Anchor Baby,[14] " Los Angeles (as of 2015) is considered the center of the maternity tourism industry. There has been a growing trend, especially amongst Asian and African visitors from Hong Kong, China, South Korea, Taiwan and Nigeria to the United States, to make use of "Birth Hotels" to secure US citizenship for their child and leave open the possibility of future immigration by the parents to the United States. The U.S. government estimates that there were 7,462 births to foreign residents in 2008 while the Center for Immigration Studies estimates that 40,000 births are born to "birth tourists" annually. Pregnant women typically spend around

$20,000 to stay in the facilities during their final months of pregnancy and an additional month to recuperate and await their new baby's U.S. passport.

According to a March 3, 2015 issue of the Wall Street Journal[14], Federal Agents in Los Angeles conducted a series of raids on three multimillion-dollar birth-tourism businesses expected to produce the biggest federal criminal case ever against the booming "anchor baby" industry. It should be noted this industry is difficult to close down because it is not illegal for a pregnant woman to travel to the U.S.

THE CONTROVERSY OF ANCHOR BABIES AND THE FOURTEENTH AMENDMENT.

A portion of **Amendment XIV** [Adopted July *28,* 1868] reads as follows:

> **Section 1** All persons born or naturalized in the United States, and ***subject to the jurisdiction thereof,*** are citizens of the United States and of the State wherein they reside.

The Colorado Alliance for Immigration Reform (CAIR), published a lengthy study of the Fourteenth Amendment as it applies to anchor babies.[15] Quoting a portion of this study:

> *"Post-Civil War reforms focused on injustices to African Americans. The 14th Amendment was ratified in 1868 to protect the rights of native-born Black Americans, whose rights were being denied as recently - freed slaves. It was-written in a manner so as to prevent state governments from ever denying citizenship to blacks born in the United States. But in 1868, the United States had no formal immigration policy, and - the authors therefore saw no need to address immigration explicitly in the amendment."*

Senator Jacob Howard worked closely with Abraham Lincoln in drafting and passing the Thirteenth Amendment to the United States Constitution, which abolished slavery. He also served on the Senate Joint Committee on Reconstruction, which drafted the Fourteenth Amendment to the United States Constitution. In 1866, Senator Jacob Howard clearly spelled out the intent of the 14th Amendment by writing:

> *"Every person born within the limits of the United States, and subject to their jurisdiction, is by virtue of natural law and national law a citizen of the United states, This will not, of course, include persons born in the United States who are foreigners, aliens, who belong to the families of ambassadors or foreign ministers accredited to the Government of the United States, but will include every other class of persons. It settles the great question of citizenship and removes all doubt as to what persons are or are not citizens of the United States. This has long been a great desideratum in the jurisprudence and legislation of this country.[15]"*

Apparently the phrase ***"subject to the jurisdiction thereof"*** is the basis for litigation and court decisions concerning the issue of citizenship by birth. CAIR contends this phrase was intended to exclude American-born persons from automatic citizenship whose allegiance to the United States was not complete.

Reference is made to **Elk v. Wilkins**, *in which* the phrase "subject to its jurisdiction" excluded from its operation "children of ministers, consuls, and citizens of foreign states born within the United States." In *Elk,* the American Indian claimant was considered not an American citizen because the law required him to be "not merely subject in some respect or degree to the jurisdiction' of the United States, but completely subject to their political jurisdiction and owing them direct and immediate allegiance."

Ignoring all the rhetoric, litigation and controversy, the fact is that being born in the United States does not guarantee the child or the parents a right to live in the U.S. An illegal family can be removed even if they have a native born child.

According to the Wikipedia article, PolitiFact of the *St. Petersburg Times,*[14] indicated the immigration benefits of having a child born in the United States are limited. Citizen children cannot sponsor parents for entry into the country until they are 21 years of age, and if the parent had ever been in the country illegally, they would have to show they had left and not returned for at least ten years;

President Reagan Amnesty & USCIS Form I-9

If an American citizen travels to a foreign country, it is certain someone would eventually check for a passport and visa. Failure to produce this documentation would ultimately lead to confinement in a foreign jail. Accordingly, it is only reasonable to expect foreigners to respect our laws the same as they would expect us to respect theirs.

During former President Ronald Reagan's term in office, it was revealed there were nearly two million persons residing in the U.S. illegally which resulted in the ***Immigration Reform and Control Act of 1986 (IRCA).*** The U.S. Citizenship and Immigration Services (**USCIS**), as part of this legislation, provided employers with an "I-9 Form" to verify legal status of employees. The employee and employer each had to fill out a separate Form I-9. To complete the I-9 process, the employer was required to obtain some form of identification to be held in the employer's files for possible review. As part of the process, a third form was provided with three lists of acceptable documents which would satisfy the requirements for proper identification.

These forms can be seen in the Appendix: Figures 1, 2 and 3.

Many employers complained this legislation unfairly required employers to engage in immigration enforcement. Employers, historically, developed their own application form which requires a social security number to enable the employer to report withholdings of Social Security, Federal and State Unemployment Insurance to various government agencies; hence, many employers felt the I-9 form was unnecessary because employees names would be matched up with social security numbers by these same governmental agencies. Unfortunately, this assumes the Social Security Administration is able to compare social security numbers with vital statistics of the various states, which, apparently, it is not able to do.

The question arises as to whether the legal requirement of swearing *"under penalty of perjury"* converts a self-employed person to an employee of the "State" with the implication of fines and possible imprisonment?

This whole procedure required some form of acceptable identification (one of which contained a picture) of each employee, and the employee/employer I-9 forms were to be held in the employer's files for possible review at a later date.

1987 President Reagan, hoping to solve the illegal alien problem in the U.S., proposed an amnesty program in which approximately 1.4 million illegal aliens took advantage of it. Common sense might lead one to believe that employer verification of legal status would eliminate the continued violation of America's immigration laws. If an illegal cannot secure a job, he cannot survive, but the better argument is that if word gets out that the U.S. is enforcing its immigration laws to include employers, then it follows the only path into America is by securing some form of legal entry.

In 2017, some 30 years after the Reagan amnesty, there are more than 11 million persons living in the U.S. who have no legal standing – so what happened? The apparent flaw with respect to *Immigration Reform and Control Act of 1986* (IRCA) is that proper enforcement required onsite inspections of the I-9 form by federal officials. Apparently, these on-site examinations, as an enforcement tool, were considered too expensive.

E-Verify: An electronic verification system.

After ten years and the continued rise of illegal immigration, it became apparent that IRCA and the I-9 form was not working. The ***Illegal Immigration Reform and Immigrant Responsibility Act of 1996*** was adopted in an effort to improve on the failing policy of interior enforcement. The new law was intended to test whether electronic verification procedures could make the existing I-9 process better by reducing document fraud and false claims of U.S. citizenship.

The federal government gradually rolled out Basic Pilot in California, Florida, Illinois, Texas, and New York, and later extended it to employers in all 50 states as a program that employers can voluntarily use. The Department of Home Security (DHS) implemented an internet version of the Basic Pilot Program nationwide in June 2004.

In addition to the requirement that employers are required to hold the I-9 data in their files for years which might, or might not, ever be reviewed, many Federal policymakers felt that an electronic employment eligibility verification system should also be required – which has come to be known as **E-Verify.** This system is administered by the U.S. Department of Homeland Security (DHS).

Unlike the IRCA I-9 forms, E-Verify is **not** mandatory except for Federal Agencies and contractors.

Policy Analysis entitled "Checking E-Verify[16]" by Alex Nowrasteh and Jim Harper of the **Cato Institute** provides an extensive analysis of E-Verify. A brief summary of some of the points covered in this analysis is as follows:

"Alabama, Arizona, Mississippi, and South Carolina, now mandate the use of E-Verify for all new hires. Those firms in Utah (15+ employees), Georgia (10+ employees), and North Carolina (25+ employees) are required to use E-Verify checks for all new hires. The states of Florida, Georgia, Idaho, Indiana, Louisiana, Missouri, Nebraska, North Carolina, Pennsylvania, Tennessee, and Virginia mandate E-Verify for all state agencies, public employers, and government contractors, while Minnesota and Colorado only require it for state contractors.

The Arizona legislature (Effective January 1, 2008) passed the Legal Arizona Workers Act (LAWA), which not only required the employer use of E-Verify for all new hires, but the law included a so-called "business death penalty." Any employer guilty of a second offense by knowingly or intentionally hiring an unauthorized immigrant would suffer a permanent revocation of the employer's licenses at the location in question thus shutting down the business.

> *To use E-Verify, employers must check new employees against govern-*
> *ment databases which would either confirm or deny an employee's right*
> *to work to legally work in the United States."*

This sounds incredibly simple; however, there are some problems beginning with the enrollment process. *The official USCIS enrollment process can be found at Figure 4 in the appendix.*

According to **"Checking E-Verify" (as noted above),** the first step in using E-Verify requires the employer to register with United States Citizenship and Immigration Services **(USCIS),** a component agency under the Department of Homeland Security **(DHS).** The employer must then agree to follow E-Verify's rules as laid out in a Memorandum of Understanding (MOU) between the employer and USCIS. Once the employer is signed up and submits the MOU online, he or she must complete an online tutorial and examination before being granted access to the system.

Once again, employers complain this process is not only complicated and time consuming but places the employer in the process of enforcing immigration law. The employer must agree to the terms of the MOU which virtually renders a self-employed person to that of State or Federal employee.

But there's more, I refer once again to the CATO Institute "Policy Analysis."

Problems with E-Verify.[16]

1. *The employer is required to hire a new worker **prior** to running a check through E-Verify. If the identity information provided is either suspected of being invalid or already in use, E-Verify flags the employee as a tenta-tive non-confirmation **(TNC).** The employer then notifies the employee. Failure to make an appeal of this TNC within 10 days would require the employer to terminate the employee.*

2. *If the worker does appeal the TNC, he or she must begin a tedious bureau-cratic review to identify and access the personal identity information that*

caused the TNC - a task made difficult by E-Verify's lack of a clear process for employees to access their information.

Because employees are not informed about which specific records, information, or data-bases are the sources of the TNC, employees may have to file Privacy Act requests with different subgroups of DHS or SSA, each of which may have been the source of the erroneously recorded information. The average response time to a Privacy Act request was last measured as 104 days in 2009.

3. *E-Verify has a strikingly high false-negative error rate that undercuts its utility. Because the heart of E-Verify is comparison between a name and Social Security number, it is often unable to detect when unauthorized workers are using false documents obtained via fraud and identity theft.*

4. *The first-level E-Verify check does not match data provided against death records. A recent report by the Social Security Administration found that approximately 6.5 million SSNs that were issued to Americans born 112 years ago or earlier do not have a death date listed in the SSA's computer database. Those SSNs can be entered into E-Verify and it would not recognize that they belong to deceased persons.*

5. *According to a USCIS-ordered audit of E-Verify conducted by the research firm Westat, an estimated 54 percent of unauthorized workers submitted to E-Verify were **incorrectly** found to be work authorized because of rampant document fraud.* Documents obtained with a valid but fraudulently used number, such as a Social Security number belonging to a recently deceased individual, will usually be returned as verified.

It would appear that no system (I-9 or E-Verify) will work unless the system is able to compare the Social Security number with "Vital Statistics" birth and death records of every State in the Union. But even with this comparison, there is no way to prevent the illegal payment in cash to illegal's because many employers consider employees and employee benefits too expensive; whereas illegals can be hired for less because they cannot complain.

As previously stated, it would appear an audit of suspected employers, at the business location, is the only realistic option to properly enforce the

Immigration Reform and Control Act of 1986; however, some have argued this procedure might be the first step toward a "police State."

THE "GANG OF EIGHT" PROPOSAL.

U.S. Congressional leaders (mostly Democrats) declared our immigration system to be "broken" and some U.S. Senators, identified as the "gang on eight," proposed (early 2013) an 844-page bill which would secure the border, allow thousands of workers into the country, and put 11 million people, who came here illegally, on a path to citizenship.

Regarding the proposal to "secure the borders" which is included in the Senate 844 page immigration reform bill, Congressman Sam Farr (D-California) commented that a fourteen foot ladder defeats a thirteen foot fence. This is true, of course, but offers little toward solving illegal immigration. American farmers and large landowners have fenced their properties for years. Some have put up "No Trespassing" signs to inform strangers that crossing the fence line could well lead to prosecution. Common sense might lead us to believe that creating a visible boundary of U.S. territory is necessary.

The thought of reading an 844 page treatise on immigration legislation which is comparable to an over-sized phone book, is overwhelming , and does anyone actually believe our immigration system is broken?,

For perspective, a Salinas Californian (July 4, 2014)[17] news item by Valentin Mendoza points out ". . .nearly 700,000 alien residents became American citizens in each of the past 10 years . . ." It would appear, based on this article, the existing immigration laws seem to be working.

To qualify for naturalization as a U.S. citizen, these 700,000 alien residents had to first secure "legal" residency by obtaining a Green Card. They must show evidence of financial responsibility, no criminal record and be in good health. After five years (three years if married to a U.S. citizen) of trouble free residency, they can apply for naturalization by filing a form N-400 or N-600 (if under the age of 18). This is followed by an interview and a citizenship test to determine the ability to speak, read and write English followed by a 100 question test on the history and government of the U.S.

After meeting all these requirements, they must take an "Oath of Allegiance" part of which reads: *". . . I absolutely and entirely renounce and abjure all allegiance and fidelity to any foreign prince, poten- tate, state, or sovereignty of whom or which I have heretofore been a subject or citizen; that I will support and defend the Constitution and laws of the United States of America against all enemies, foreign and domestic. . ."*

This "Oath" means these newly sworn citizens place the sovereign inter- ests of the United States as their top priority over any such obligations they might have for any other country. Accordingly, it can be assumed, an illegal alien within the boundaries of our nation has made no such commitment, nor, it would appear, is he entitled to a place ahead of all those who are seek- ing legal citizenship.

The Washington Post published an article by Krissan Williams (June 27, 2007) concerning Jeffrey West[18], an American who lives in Texas but runs an office in Monterrey, Mexico. For $160 he will do all the visa paper work required by the Federal Guest Worker Program "H-2A" for those foreign per- sons who wish to work in the United States. At that time he was maintaining a secure data base of more than 20,000 Mexican men and women who were/ are working in the U.S.

The up side is all these workers are documented and legal in accordance to provisions of the U.S. Immigration laws. The down side is that H-2A requires employers to provide living accommodations and transportation for those workers who are unable to return each day to Mexico. Some might recall the H-2A "Bracero" program of the 1960's in which thousands of field hands worked in California. But the restrictions of this particular program simply will not work for many of California's undocumented workers particularly those who have lived here for years and have raised a family in their own home. Even so, there are other guest worker programs on the books. The H-1B visa and L-1 visa programs have documented one million guest workers in the U.S. and that was in 2007.

It seems the existing immigration laws have provisions to handle tempo- rary workers without resorting to an 844 page boondoggle.

Border problems.

A September 26, 2014 Associated Press article[19] claimed that, of the approximate 59,000 young families caught illegally crossing our southern border and were allowed to enter the US, about 70 percent (or an estimated 41,000) never showed up weeks later for their follow up appointments. With this kind of lax and porous treatment of incoming illegals, why would any terrorist group recruit an American citizen when they can send a seemingly innocent young person across the border seeking asylum without fear they will be hunted down for failure to keep an appointment.

Federal Enforcement of Immigration Laws confusing.

Arizona SB 1070, signed into law by Governor Jan Brewer on April 23, 2010, was at that time, the broadest and strictest anti-illegal immigration measure in recent history. Arizona was criticized for "racial profiling" because a traffic ticket could result in an undocumented immigrant being handed over to federal authorities. It received national and international attention and spurred considerable controversy. The law was modified by Arizona House ·Bill 2162 within a week of its signing with the goal of addressing some of these concerns.

U.S. federal law requires all aliens over the age of 14 who remain in the United States for longer than 30 days to register with the U.S. government, and to have registration documents in their possession at all times; violation of this requirement is a federal misdemeanor crime.

The Arizona act made it a state misdemeanor crime for an alien to be in Arizona without carrying the required documents and required that state law enforcement officers attempt to determine an individual's immigration status during a "lawful stop, detention or arrest," if there was reasonable suspicion that the individual was an illegal immigrant. The law barred state or local officials or agencies from restricting enforcement of federal immigration laws, and imposed penalties on those sheltering, hiring and transporting unregistered aliens. The paragraph on intent in the legislation says it embodies an "attrition through enforcement" doctrine.

The U.S. Supreme Court struck down parts of Arizona's immigration law, but upheld the provision which required police officers to check the immigration status of people they stopped and reasonably suspected as being in the country illegally.

California responded with the "Anti-Arizona" bill or officially named the "Trust Act," AB 1081, introduced by Tom Ammiano, a San Francisco Assemblyman. Incredibly, the thrust of this legislation encouraged local authorities to ignore an agreement with the Obama administration allowing federal immigration agents to review fingerprints under the "Secure Communities program" in order to track down and pick up every deportable immigrant arrested by local police. Instead, this bill proposed that, after paying fines or resolving some sort of "minor" offense, a perpetrator should be turned loose without waiting for any sort of review by federal immigration authorities.

Apparently, California Legislators concluded there is nothing wrong with violating U.S. immigration laws so long as these illegal aliens refrain from killing someone, or otherwise engaging in a major felony. This bill passed both houses of the State Legislature but was vetoed by Governor Jerry Brown.

Never-the-less, California continues to encourage local authorities to ignore an agreement with the Obama administration allowing federal immigration agents to review fingerprints under the "Secure Communities Program."

In contradiction to a long standing rule of federal law, Californian Assemblyman Luis Allejo (D-Salinas) introduced AB 60 which would allow drivers licenses to be issued to persons unable to prove they have a legal right to be in the U.S.

To overcome existing law section 12801 (c) (1) of the proposed legislation reads as follows: "An applicant who is unable to provide satisfactory proof that his or her presence in the United States is authorized under federal law may sign an affidavit ~~under penalty of perjury~~ attesting that he or she is both ineligible for a social security account number and unable to submit satisfactory proof that his or her presence in the United States is ~~unauthorized~~ *authorized* under federal law." It should be noted this affidavit is not a public record, and Section 12801 (2) "The submission of this affidavit shall be accepted by the department (DMV) in lieu of a social security account number."

Because "under penalty of perjury" is deleted from this legislation, applicants can offer false statements without penalty – indeed, it encourages a loose treatment of fact. Someone who knows, beyond a reasonable doubt, he is in the country illegally can truthfully state he cannot provide satisfactory proof his presence in the U.S. is authorized under federal law and this affidavit also satisfies the social security requirement.

California is also a participant in the Federal "Motor-Voter" law which allows automatic voter registration when obtaining or renewing a driver's license. There was concern that illegals might, under terms of this Federal law, be allowed to vote. State officials denied this possibility because the driver's license issued was different and specially marked. Never-the-less, this remains a concern because, on June 17, 2013, the U.S. Supreme Court, on a 7-2 vote regarding an Arizona "proof-of-citizenship" law, ruled that States cannot demand proof of citizenship from people registering to vote in federal elections without first obtaining permission from the "Elections Citizens Committee" or a federal court; thus complicating efforts in Arizona and other states to bar voting by people who are in the country illegally. ***This ruling was limited to those persons registering by use of a federal form.***

Regarding an Associated Press article (June 18, 2013)[20] Matt Roberts, a spokesman for Arizona Secretary of State Ken Bennett, was quoted as stating that less than 5 percent of people registering to vote in Arizona use the federal form. The rest register through the state system which means they will continue to be asked to provide proof of citizenship when signing up to vote.

The question arises: "*Since California already has allowed illegals to acquire a driver's license, what prevents them from registering to vote?*" In response to this question it was pointed out that the driver's license issued to an undocumented applicant is distinctively marked to prevent confusion with a regular driver's license which would prevent an illegal from registering to vote.

"*What prevents an undocumented driver from registering to vote by choosing* the *less burdensome federal form which does not allow voting registrars to ask for* 'proof-of-citizenship'?" There is no apparent solution to this problem nor the fact that a distinctively marked driver's license would, in fact, identify a driver as a probable illegal alien.

In addition to allowing illegals to acquire a driver's license, California, desperate for cheap labor, has abrogated or otherwise ignored immigration requirements and provided many other benefits to undocumented immigrants. The Medic-aid provisions have widened to include so-called "undocumented" immigrants as well as free medical and grants "Dreamers" (children of illegals). Considering all the benefits awarded to the illegal population in California, why would anyone want to mess this thing up by becoming a citizen?

SANCTUARY CITIES – A NATION DIVIDED.

Following the election of Donald Trump, U.S. cities have lined up by the dozens and announced that they will not assist the federal government in the deportation of illegals. Even Universities have declared themselves off-limits to federal law.

It is difficult to understand why a city or a State like California would declare itself a "Sanctuary" for persons who have placed themselves in the United States in violation of federal immigration laws. Some have reasoned that an illegal alien should not be removed by the U.S. Immigration and Enforcement officers (ICE) unless they are guilty of some sort of major crime.

California is using the Tenth Amendment, the "States' Rights" nullification doctrine, to become a sanctuary state and defy federal law as well - but is it constitutional?

Harold Pease, Ph. D is a syndicated columnist and an expert on the United States Constitution, published an article summarizing the concept of nullification as it applies to Sanctuary Cities and States Rights.[21] An amended portion of this article reads as follows:

"The problem is immigration is clearly left to the federal government as part of the U.S. Constitution. Article I, Section 8, Clause 4 gives the federal government the right, *'To establish an uniform Rule at Naturalization.'* Moreover, eight of the 18 clauses listed as the powers of Congress deal with national security and border security defines even the existence of a nation. The Constitution puts an end to the issue in Article 6: ***'This Constitution, and the Laws of the United States which shall be made in Pursuance thereat ... shall be the supreme Law at the Land; and the judges in every State shall be bound thereby, any Thing in the Constitution or Laws at any State to the Contrary notwithstanding.'. . .*** Every mayor has taken a solemn oath *'to preserve, protect and defend the Constitution of the United States.' The* existence of sanctuary cities is as clear a constitutional violation as exists.'"

The Nullification Confusion: The Tenth Amendment to the U.S. Constitution:

"The powers not delegated to the United States by the Constitution nor prohibited by it to the States, are reserved to the States respectively, or to the people."

Because the legalization of Marijuana in several U.S. states is based upon the principle of "States Rights" as defined in the Tenth Amendment, most people have assumed the various States could also ignore Federal Immigration laws as part of the same nullification doctrine. This idea, of course, is false – so what is the difference?

A good example would be Prohibition: which made it illegal to manufacture, store in barrels or bottles, transport, sell, possess or consume alcohol including alcoholic beverages.

This law was in effect in the U.S. between 1920 to 1933, and yet no state or city attempted to claim nullification due to State's Rights – why?

It might be wishful thinking to conclude those were different times and maybe people had more respect for Federal Laws. The fact is that prohibition was put in place by the 18th Amendment and became a part of the U.S. Constitution. This meant that it was a power specifically delegated to the Federal Government and not subject to States Rights.

The Federal Law prohibiting the use of marijuana is not provided for in the Constitution and is, therefore, vulnerable to claims of nullification.

The Sanctuary Cities concept does not fall into the same category as marijuana - as Doctor Harold Pease points out: ***"immigration is clearly left to the federal government as part of the U.S. Constitution. Article I, Section 8, Clause 4."***

When President Trump threatened to terminate federal funds to those cities claiming sanctuary, the city officials, disregarding the thought they might be a bit hypocritical, voiced their alarm as if the President had the nerve to cut off their federal funds because of their defiance of Federal Law. .

I have never liked the idea of a law requiring me to put on a seatbelt; but, if I don't agree with this provision of the law, do I get the luxury of ignoring it? And if I am caught ignoring this law, will the court cancel my ticket when I explain that I have always opposed this law?

According to my law book: ***Accessory after the fact*** – "One, who, knowing a felony to have been committed by another, aids the felon to avoid punishment."

Of course, crossing our border without permission is (apparently) not considered a felony – unless they are caught a second time. Because many sanctuary cities have extended their protection to include persons who have been arrested for criminal acts, a question arises: "Does this protection qualify them as an *Accessory After The Fact?*"

Currently Legislators are proposing the State of California ought to secede from the Union because President Trump and the "Feds" are threatening to withhold funding to so-called *Sanctuary Cities.*

Referring to the chapter called "Crito" (of Plato's "Apology"), Socrates was offered an opportunity to escape to a neighboring country. He responded by asking, ***"Do you think that a state can exist and not be overthrown, in which the decisions of the law are of no force, and are disregarded and set at nought by private individuals?"***

Voter Apathy.

Concerning the issue of Sanctuary Cities and possible secession from the Union of the United States, one wonders how it came to pass that some elected officials seem to feel they can ignore federal laws. Obviously, California legislators have come to realize a huge percentage of the voting public has lost interest in political issues and no longer hold their local representative responsible his voting record. This voter apathy is nothing new. Nearly 93 million eligible voters for the highly controversial November, 2016 presidential election failed to vote, and another 20 million-plus of voting age did not bother to register. As a result approximately 60 percent or 138,884,643 out of a possible 231,556,622 eligible population of American voters, selected this nation's next president.

"The price of Liberty is eternal vigilance . . ." –Frank Birch. This is a lesson which appears to be lost.

Illegals: The other side of the story.

According to the Wikipedia article (Economic impact of Illegal immigrants in the U.S.[22]): the IRS estimates that about 6 million unauthorized immigrants file individual income tax returns each year, and the Congressional Budget Office indicates that between 50 percent and 75 percent of unauthorized immigrants pay federal, state, and local taxes.

Illegal immigrants are estimated to pay in about $7 billion per year into Social Security; additionally, they occupy over three million dwellings and produce $150-billion in economic activity each year which supports the US economy and helps to create new jobs.

With regard to Social Security taxes, illegal immigrants pay social security payroll taxes but are not eligible for benefits. A Standard & Poor's 2006 analysis indicated the U.S. Social Security Administration allocates roughly $6 billion to $7 billion of Social Security contributions in an "earnings suspense file" each year resulting from W-2 tax forms that cannot be matched to the correct Social Security number. The vast majority of these numbers are attributable to illegal workers who will never claim their benefits. For 2010, the Social Security Administration estimated that illegal immigrants and their employers paid $13 billion in social security (OASDI) payroll taxes.

It has been suggested by those in support of "undocumented immigrants" that, because illegals pay taxes, they are not a financial burden to the U.S.

taxpayer and that they perform jobs that Americans simply do not want to do. Farmers also complain they are unable to obtain sufficient help at harvest time to bring in their crops.

Many California cities, in an apparent justification for offering sanctuary to illegals, indicate a severe lack of police support because the illegal constituency fear they may be deported.

ILLEGAL IMMIGRATION: *THE PRICE WE PAY.*

Disclaimer: I must confess to the alarming inability to gather accurate data concerning monetary costs related to illegal aliens in the U.S. Don't get me wrong – there is plenty of information available on the internet or local and national syndicated news services, but much of it is exaggerated and simply not true.

The Federation for American Immigration Reform **"FAIR"** issued a report entitled "***The Fiscal Burden of Illegal Immigration on United States Taxpayers (3013)[23]***" in which they issued five Key Findings:

KEY FINDINGS

- Illegal immigration costs U.S. taxpayers about **$113 billion a year** at the federal, state and local level. The bulk of the costs - some $84 billion - are absorbed by state and local governments.
- The annual outlay that illegal aliens cost U.S. taxpayers is an average amount per native-headed household of $1,117. The fiscal impact per household varies considerably because the greatest share of the burden falls on state and local taxpayers whose burden depends on the size of the illegal alien population in that locality
- Education for the children of illegal aliens constitutes the single largest cost to taxpayers, at an annual price tag of nearly $52 billion. Nearly all of those costs are absorbed by state and local governments.
- At the federal level, about one-third of outlays are matched by tax collections from illegal aliens. At the state and local level, an average of

less than 5 percent of the public costs associated with illegal immigration is recouped through taxes collected from illegal aliens.

- Most illegal aliens do not pay income taxes. Among those who do, much of the revenues collected are refunded to the illegal aliens when they file tax returns. Many are also claiming tax credits resulting in payments from the U.S. Treasury.

Not included in these "findings," California law enforcement officials complain they are unable to get help from undocumented immigrants because they fear deportation; however, most cities provide a telephone contact number so that witnesses may reveal police related information on an anonymous basis. The real problem is not limited to illegal immigrants. In those areas where gang activity and criminal behavior dominate the neighborhood, fear of retaliation is the real threat and is not limited to illegal aliens.

IMMIGRATION ENFORCEMENT: TWO PROBLEMS.

There is little doubt that population and immigration are part of the same problem. According to the Wikipedia report *"Demographics of the United States,*[8]*"* the estimated fertility rate in the United States for 2014 is 1.86 children per woman, which is below the replacement fertility rate of approximately 2.1. The US fertility rate was lower than that of France (2.01), Australia (1.93) and the United Kingdom (1.92); however, ***US population growth is among the highest in industrialized countries because of the massive legal and illegal immigration levels.***

Clearly, if this nation wants to stabilize its population, it must control immigration; however, no legislation to stem the flow of illegal immigration will work unless some provision is made to enforce the law.

The I-9 Form, as mentioned previously, has failed because it requires onsite audits which, apparently, is either too expensive to consider or legislators fear employer back-lash with accusations of creating a police state.

E-Verify has little impact because effective enforcement can only be accomplished if the Social Security Agency and/or governmental agencies handling unemployment insurance is able to compare social security numbers with birth and death records to provide more accurate information.

PROBLEM NUMBER 1.

A national data base which compares social security numbers with birth and death records would appear to be necessary for both the I-9 form and E-Verify to work.

Looking back to the 1930's, when President Franklin D. Roosevelt proposed Social Security as a national retirement system, one of the largest objections to the program was the issuance of a social security number. It was argued that this would be the beginning of a controlled society much like George Orwell's 1984 where people would be given numbers and surveilled by Big Brother.

It was June 8, 2013, when an article by Clive Irving entitled *"Behold the NSA's Dark Star: the Utah Data Center"*[24] appeared on the internet which disclosed that billions of dollars had gone into creating a cyber-intelligence facility for the National Security Agency (NSA). According to this article: *"There's no official explanation of the Utah Data Center's real mission, except that it's the largest of a network of data farms including sites in Colorado, Georgia and Maryland . . .Of course, the U.S. is still far from being the police state that East Germany was. . "*

The "Dark Star" article was followed by additional editorials including an Associated Press article by Gregory Katz[25] "Guardian making splash in U.S." The Guardian article identified secret surveillance operations in the U.S. including the collection of telephone records from Verizon of millions of U.S. customers.

These articles coupled with accusations the Patriot Act violated the Fourth Amendment rights: "The right of the people to be secure in their persons, houses, papers, and effects, against unreasonable searches and seizures, shall not be violated, and no warrants shall issue but upon probable cause . . ." became a major issue and remains unresolved to this day.

Any suggestion of converting NSA's Dark Star to comparing social security information with vital statistics of all 50 states would appear to be a non-starter because of controversial police state implications.

PROBLEM NUMBER 2.

Effective enforcement to prevent the huge influx of illegal immigrants is logically dependent upon the cooperation and support of the public at large. It is very probable that the original *Immigration Reform and Control Act of 1986* was never intended to result in on-site audits but the mere act of filling out the I-9 form and the willing cooperation of employers would stop the influx of illegals into the U.S. Realistically, if an illegal cannot secure a job, then he or she cannot survive and would be discouraged from illegal entry.

The problem is that a large portion of society seems unconcerned that millions of persons residing in the U.S. are here in violation of the law and the fact their allegiance belongs to a foreign nation.

California, desperate for cheap labor, has abrogated or otherwise ignored immigration requirements under the guise of "States Rights." In addition to allowing illegals to acquire a driver's license, Medic-aid provisions have been widened to include those who are "unable to submit satisfactory proof that his or her presence in the United States is *authorized.*" Moreover, California provides free health benefits and educational grants to children of undocumented residents.

"Why should anyone become a U.S. citizen if there are more benefits available to non-citizens than there are to the rest of the nation?"

CHAPTER 9

Final Remarks: Population, what is reasonable?

————

IT IS PROBABLY SAFE TO say that when a country's occupants starve to death for lack of food, a reasonable solution to that problem would be to reduce the population to a level that matches the food available. This, of course, is common sense.

THE IDEAL SOLUTION.

To engage in wishful thinking, why not go back to the good old days when the human condition allowed a friendly relationship with others in the community and an individual believed his life has meaning and purpose.

If common sense is utilized, population numbers should be in balance with nature so that other creatures are allowed to survive. Once the ideal population numbers are established, Immigration would only be allowed to fill in vacancies created by death or disaster not to exceed the predetermined population count.

Realistically, these ideas will never be seriously considered; however, the beginning of a solution can be had if the United States would enforce immigration laws and limit that portion of population growth.

POPULATION – IMMIGRATION
REFERENCES

1. Genesis: The Holy Bible, The Old Testament being the version set forth in 1611 A.D.

2. World Population Clock http://www.worldometers.info/worldpopulation In addition to the actual population clock, sub-sections of this web site provides world population statistics.

3. http://www.worldpopulationstatistics.com which is a part of the World Population Clock web site.

4. Fresno Bee Saturday, May 7, 2005 by Mark Grossi: ***"Cows emit more organic gas than cars, studies say,"***

5. Associated Press article, September 5, 2017, by Cathy Bussewitz: ***Fear of robots taking jobs spurs a bold idea.***

6. Wikipedia : One Child Policy https://en.wikipedia.org/wiki/One-child_policy

7. Plagues and Pandemics: Wikipedia **https://en.wikipedia.org/wiki/Pandemic**

8. Demographics of the United States Wikipedia: https://wikipedia.org/wiki/Demographics

9. Vaccinations required by law. **Vaccines.org/view.php**

10. CAR T-cell therapy **www.webmd.com/cancer/news**

11. Monterey Herald June 28, 2017, by Tom Leyde: ***Monterey County Crop Values Down in 2016***

12. Associated Press article (June 23, 2014) by Alicia A. Caldwell *"Few immediate consequences for immigrant children."*

13. Wikipedia: *"Anchor Babies"*https://wikipedia.org/wiki/Anchorbabies

14. Wikipedia: "Anchor Baby" https://wikipedia.org/wiki/Anchor_baby

15. Colorado Alliance for Immigration Reform (CAIR): *"Anchor babies, birthright citizenship, and the 14ᵗʰ Amendment"* (**http://www.cairco.org/issues/anchor-babies**).

16. *"Checking E-Verify"* Cato Institute: Policy Analysis dated July 7, 2015 **https//object.cato.org/sites/cato.org/files/pubs/pdf/pa775_1.pdf**

17. *"Happy birthday America! Welcome, new Americans!* Salinas Californian July 4, 2014

18. The Washington Post article (June 27, 2007) by Krissan Williams: *Jeffrey West*

19. Associated Press, September 26, 2014 by Alicia A. Caldwell: *US: Many immigrant families fail to report to agents"*

20. Associated Press, June 18, 2013 by Jesse J. Holland: *Arizona's proof-of-citizenship voting law ruled illegal*

21. *California Uses Nullification Doctrine to Protect Illegals:* (dated 12/19/2016) by Harold Pease, Ph.D. https://en,wikipedia,org/wiki/immigration_to_the_United_States

22. *Wikipedia*: *Economic impact of illegal immigrants in the United States* https://en.wikipedia.org/wiki/Economic-impact-of-illegal-immigrants-in-the-United-States

23. FAIR report: ***The Fiscal Burden of Illegal Immigration on United States Taxpayers (3013)*** – **http://www.fairus.org/publications/the-fiscal-burden-of -illegal-immigration-on-united-states**

24. The Daily Beast article (June 8, 2013) by Clive Irving: ***Behold the NSA's Dark Star: the Utah Data Center.***

25. Associated Press article (June 8, 2013) by Gregory Katz: ***Guardian making splash in U.S.***

Employment Eligibility Verification	USCIS
Department of Homeland Security	Form I-9
U.S. Citizenship and Immigration Services	OMB No. 1615-0047
	Expires 08/31/2019

▶ START HERE: Read instructions carefully before completing this form. The instructions must be available, either in paper or electronically, during completion of this form. Employers are liable for errors in the completion of this form.

ANTI-DISCRIMINATION NOTICE: It is illegal to discriminate against work-authorized individuals. Employers **CANNOT** specify which document(s) an employee may present to establish employment authorization and identity. The refusal to hire or continue to employ an individual because the documentation presented has a future expiration date may also constitute illegal discrimination.

Section 1. Employee Information and Attestation *(Employees must complete and sign Section 1 of Form I-9 no later than the first day of employment, but not before accepting a job offer.)*

Last Name *(Family Name)*	First Name *(Given Name)*		Middle Initial	Other Last Names Used *(if any)*	
Address *(Street Number and Name)*	Apt. Number	City or Town		State	ZIP Code
Date of Birth *(mm/dd/yyyy)*	U.S. Social Security Number	Employee's E-mail Address		Employee's Telephone Number	

I am aware that federal law provides for imprisonment and/or fines for false statements or use of false documents in connection with the completion of this form.

I attest, under penalty of perjury, that I am (check one of the following boxes):

☐ 1. A citizen of the United States

☐ 2. A noncitizen national of the United States *(See instructions)*

☐ 3. A lawful permanent resident   (Alien Registration Number/USCIS Number)

☐ 4. An alien authorized to work   until (expiration date, if applicable, mm/dd/yyyy)
　　　Some aliens may write "N/A" in the expiration date field. *(See instructions)*

Aliens authorized to work must provide only one of the following document numbers to complete Form I-9. An Alien Registration Number/USCIS Number OR Form I-94 Admission Number OR Foreign Passport Number.

	QR Code - Section 1 Do Not Write In This Space

1. Alien Registration Number/USCIS Number

OR

2. Form I-94 Admission Number

OR

3. Foreign Passport Number

　　Country of Issuance

Signature of Employee	Today's Date *(mm/dd/yyyy)*

Preparer and/or Translator Certification (check one):

☐ I did not use a preparer or translator.　　☐ A preparer(s) and/or translator(s) assisted the employee in completing Section 1

(Fields below must be completed and signed when preparers and/or translators assist an employee in completing Section 1.)

I attest, under penalty of perjury, that I have assisted in the completion of Section 1 of this form and that to the best of my knowledge the information is true and correct.

Signature of Preparer or Translator	Today's Date *(mm/dd/yyyy)*
Last Name *(Family Name)*	First Name *(Given Name)*
Address *(Street Number and Name)*	City or Town	State	ZIP Code

🛑 *Employer Completes Next Page* 🛑

Figure 1. Employee Form

Employment Eligibility Verification
Department of Homeland Security
U.S. Citizenship and Immigration Services

USCIS
Form I-9
OMB No. 1615-0047
Expires 08/31/2019

Section 2. Employer or Authorized Representative Review and Verification

(Employers or their authorized representative must complete and sign Section 2 within 3 business days of the employee's first day of employment. You must physically examine one document from List A OR a combination of one document from List B and one document from List C as listed on the "Lists of Acceptable Documents.")

Employee Info from Section 1	Last Name *(Family Name)*	First Name *(Given Name)*	M.I.	Citizenship/Immigration Status

List A	OR	List B	AND	List C
Identity and Employment Authorization		Identity		Employment Authorization

Document Title	Document Title	Document Title
Issuing Authority	Issuing Authority	Issuing Authority
Document Number	Document Number	Document Number
Expiration Date *(if any)(mm/dd/yyyy)*	Expiration Date *(if any)(mm/dd/yyyy)*	Expiration Date *(if any)(mm/dd/yyyy)*

Document Title	
Issuing Authority	Additional Information
Document Number	
Expiration Date *(if any)(mm/dd/yyyy)*	
Document Title	QR Code - Sections 2 & 3 Do Not Write In This Space
Issuing Authority	
Document Number	
Expiration Date *(if any)(mm/dd/yyyy)*	

Certification: I attest, under penalty of perjury, that (1) I have examined the document(s) presented by the above-named employee, (2) the above-listed document(s) appear to be genuine and to relate to the employee named, and (3) to the best of my knowledge the employee is authorized to work in the United States.

The employee's first day of employment *(mm/dd/yyyy)*: _____ *(See instructions for exemptions)*

Signature of Employer or Authorized Representative	Today's Date*(mm/dd/yyyy)*	Title of Employer or Authorized Representative
Last Name of Employer or Authorized Representative	First Name of Employer or Authorized Representative	Employer's Business or Organization Name
Employer's Business or Organization Address (Street Number and Name)	City or Town	State	ZIP Code

Section 3. Reverification and Rehires *(To be completed and signed by employer or authorized representative.)*

A. New Name *(if applicable)*			B. Date of Rehire *(if applicable)*
Last Name *(Family Name)*	First Name *(Given Name)*	Middle Initial	Date *(mm/dd/yyyy)*

C. If the employee's previous grant of employment authorization has expired, provide the information for the document or receipt that establishes continuing employment authorization in the space provided below.

Document Title	Document Number	Expiration Date *(if any) (mm/dd/yyyy)*

I attest, under penalty of perjury, that to the best of my knowledge, this employee is authorized to work in the United States, and if the employee presented document(s), the document(s) I have examined appear to be genuine and to relate to the individual.

Signature of Employer or Authorized Representative	Today's Date *(mm/dd/yyyy)*	Name of Employer or Authorized Representative

Form I-9 11/14/2016 N

Page 2 of 3

Figure 2. Employer Form

LISTS OF ACCEPTABLE DOCUMENTS
All documents must be UNEXPIRED

Employees may present one selection from List A
or a combination of one selection from List B and one selection from List C

LIST A	LIST B	LIST C
Documents that Establish Both Identity and Employment Authorization	Documents that Establish Identity	Documents that Establish Employment Authorization
OR		**AND**
1. U.S. Passport or U.S. Passport Card	1. Driver's license or ID card issued by a State or outlying possession of the United States provided it contains a photograph or information such as name, date of birth, gender, height, eye color, and address	1. A Social Security Account Number card, unless the card includes one of the following restrictions: (1) NOT VALID FOR EMPLOYMENT (2) VALID FOR WORK ONLY WITH INS AUTHORIZATION (3) VALID FOR WORK ONLY WITH DHS AUTHORIZATION
2. Permanent Resident Card or Alien Registration Receipt Card (Form I-551)		
3. Foreign passport that contains a temporary I-551 stamp or temporary I-551 printed notation on a machine-readable immigrant visa	2. ID card issued by federal, state or local government agencies or entities, provided it contains a photograph or information such as name, date of birth, gender, height, eye color, and address	2. Certification of Birth Abroad issued by the Department of State (Form FS-545)
4. Employment Authorization Document that contains a photograph (Form I-766)	3. School ID card with a photograph	3. Certification of Report of Birth issued by the Department of State (Form DS-1350)
5. For a nonimmigrant alien authorized to work for a specific employer because of his or her status:	4. Voter's registration card	
a. Foreign passport; and	5. U.S. Military card or draft record	4. Original or certified copy of birth certificate issued by a State, county, municipal authority, or territory of the United States bearing an official seal
b. Form I-94 or Form I-94A that has the following:	6. Military dependent's ID card	
(1) The same name as the passport; and	7. U.S. Coast Guard Merchant Mariner Card	
(2) An endorsement of the alien's nonimmigrant status as long as that period of endorsement has not yet expired and the proposed employment is not in conflict with any restrictions or limitations identified on the form	8. Native American tribal document	5. Native American tribal document
	9. Driver's license issued by a Canadian government authority	6. U.S. Citizen ID Card (Form I-197)
	For persons under age 18 who are unable to present a document listed above:	7. Identification Card for Use of Resident Citizen in the United States (Form I-179)
6. Passport from the Federated States of Micronesia (FSM) or the Republic of the Marshall Islands (RMI) with Form I-94 or Form I-94A indicating nonimmigrant admission under the Compact of Free Association Between the United States and the FSM or RMI	10. School record or report card	8. Employment authorization document issued by the Department of Homeland Security
	11. Clinic, doctor, or hospital record	
	12. Day-care or nursery school record	

Examples of many of these documents appear in Part 8 of the Handbook for Employers (M-274).

Refer to the instructions for more information about acceptable receipts.

Figure 3. Acceptable Documents

U.S. Citizenship and Immigration Services

Figure 4. E-verify Process

THE ENROLLMENT PROCESS

When you enroll your company in E-Verify, you need to tell us some basic information about your company and agree to the rules of our program. During the enrollment process, you will:

- Answer four yes/no questions to determine your access method
- Select your organization designation if your company is a federal contractor or other special category
- Review, acknowledge, and agree to the memorandum of understanding (MOU)
- Enter your company details
- Enter your North American Industry Classification System (NAICS) Code
- Provide hiring site information
- Register E-Verify program administrator(s)
- Review and certify the information you entered
- Print your electronically signed MOU

1. Visit Enrollment Website and Accept Terms

You can enroll in E-Verify through the enrollment website. You must read and agree to the terms explained before you may continue. Then review the <u>enrollment check list</u> and be sure you have all of the required information before you click "Begin E-Verify Enrollment."

2. Determine Your Access Method

An <u>access method</u> provides companies with different functions within E-Verify. The four access methods are employer, E-Verify employer agent, corporate administrator, and Web services.

E-Verify will guide you through four questions to help determine which access method is right for your company. Read the questions carefully because errors can delay us from approving your company's enrollment. Each access method includes an explanation and a question for you to answer. You'll need to answer all four questions in order to continue.

3. Review and Confirm Access Method

E-Verify gives you an opportunity to review your enrollment answers and to confirm that the access method selected fits your company's needs.

4. Select Your Organization Designation

Certain types of organizations have unique E-Verify requirements so it's important for us to know if your company is a federal contractor with or without the Federal Acquisition Regulation (FAR) E-Verify clause or a federal, state or local government organization. If you select one of those categories, you may be asked additional questions related to that category. If none of those categories applies to your company, you should select 'None of these categories apply.'

5. Review and Agree to the Memorandum of Understanding (MOU)

Review your company's obligations as explained in the MOU and indicate whether that you agree with the terms. You will be given the opportunity to download a copy of your electronically signed MOU at the end of the enrollment process.

6. Enter MOU Signatory Information

Enter the contact information of the person who electronically signed the MOU on the preceding page. You're also given the opportunity to designate this person as an E-Verify program administrator.

7. Enter Company Information

Enter your company details, including your company's name, parent organization, physical verification location, mailing address, employer identification number and total number of employees. If you are enrolling your company in E-Verify employer access and you would like to link this account to an existing corporate account, you may do so.

8. Enter or Select North American Industry Classification System (NAICS) Code

Enter the first three digits of your company's NAICS code if you know it. If you do not know your company's NAICS code, you can leave the NAICS code field blank and click "Generate NAICS code."

9. Provide Hiring Site Information

Enter the number of hiring sites that will participate in E-Verify for each state. Do not include sites that will not participate in E-Verify. Remember, while you are free to choose E-Verify participation on a site-by-site basis, your company must use E-Verify for all newly hired employees at each participating site.

10. Register E-Verify Program Administrators

During enrollment, you can register as many program administrators as you would like, however, you must register at least one. If you indicated earlier that your MOU signatory should also be a program administrator, that person is listed though you can choose to add more. After enrollment, your program administrator(s) can register general users and additional program administrators.

11. Review and Certify Information

Please review the information you've provided because errors can cause delays in approving your enrollment. If you need to change any information, you can do so before you certify and submit your enrollment.

12. Print Signed Memorandum of Understanding (MOU)

The enrollment confirmation page confirms that we have received your enrollment information. Before you go, be sure to print a. copy of the Memorandum of Understanding (MOU) you electronically signed. We recommend you share it with your human resources, legal counsel and other appropriate staff.